The 3 Rs

Ranting
Rhyming
Revolting

By Janine Booth

H P

For more information, poems, articles and more, visit:
www.janinebooth.com
Website design by Peter North @prnorth

Twitter @JanineBooth
Facebook: www.facebook.com/JanineBoothTheBigJ

For enquiries, including inviting Janine to perform her poetry,
contact **janine.booth@btopenworld.com**

Autism Equality at Work:
removing barriers and challenging discrimination
(Jessica Kingsley Publishers, forthcoming April 2016)

Mostly Hating Tories:
poems by Janine Booth
(Hastings Press, 2015)

Autism in the Workplace:
a handbook for trade unionists
(e-published by the Trade Union Congress, 2014)

Plundering London Underground:
New Labour, private capital and public service 1997–2010
(Merlin Press, 2013)

Guilty and Proud of It:
Poplar's rebel councillors and guardians 1919–1926
(Merlin Press, 2009)

Comrades and Sisters:
women and the struggle for liberation
(Workers' Liberty, 1999)

Radical Chains:
sexuality and class politics
(Workers' Liberty, 1999)

ranting rhyming revolting

Published by The Hastings Press
ISBN 978-1-904109-30-3
Book design by the author

about the author

Janine Booth was a 'ranting poet' in the 1980s under the name The Big J, took a break of 25 years, and returned to performing poetry on stage in summer 2014.

She has performed at London poetry nights including Jawdance, Loose Muse, Hammer and Tongue, Technically Speaking and Paper Tiger Poetry; around the UK, including in Brighton, Wigan, Peterborough, Tolpuddle and Doncaster; at music gigs as well as spoken word events; at festivals, political and campaign events; and internationally in Paris, Toronto, New York City and Berlin.

Janine's poems have been published in various journals and websites, including Screaming Violets, Poetry24, Solidarity, Stand Up and Spit, Hastings Independent, Freedom, Women's Fightback and TenFootCity.

Janine is an active trade unionist, Marxist and socialist-feminist. She tutors and speaks on various political and historical subjects, and sometimes slips a poem into her speeches. And she has a day job on the railway.

ranting rhyming revolting

contents

ranting rhyming revolting

red brick dreams

If I could build the world from LEGO bricks
The clean-lined architecture would delight
We'd build for function and construct for kicks
Each beautiful creative studded site
If I could build the world from LEGO bricks
I would not let one small set hoard them all
To build monstrosities to make them rich
While others wait in hope for tiles to fall
    If I could build the world from LEGO bricks
    I'd prise apart the bastions of power
    And use that handy orange lever stick
    To flick away the walls of tyrants' tower
    If I rebuilt the world with LEGO bricks
    It'd be a commonwealth of minifigs

red-hearted man

for Brian Munro, 1968-2014

How are you feeling today, my friend?
'Pretty shit', you said
And how do you feel at another year's end?
'Now I feel nothing – I'm dead'

You said you'd be molecules when you're gone
To the earth and the sky wide and far
You left us your words and your memory fires on
Your loved ones just look to the stars

You're with us on picket lines, like Joe Hill
You're there on the road that we tread
You're there in the branch and the workplace still
'Get out and organise', you said

Your life was the march towards a brighter light
From your youth to your hospice bed
You've passed us the gloves to keep up the fight
'Don't fuck it up', you said

Read books, practise instruments, use what you're taught
Live your full life while you can
For here lies a man whose life was too short
Here lies a red-hearted man

Here lies a gardener, a diner, a cook
Here lies a travelling fan
A father, a lover – of a wine and a book
Yes, here lies a red-hearted man

four leaf clover

The child amongst us
Finds a four leaf clover
On the woman's grave next to her dad's.

The cynic amongst us says
It wasn't very lucky for her, was it?

The herbologist amongst us observes that
It's not a four leaf clover
It's wild sorrel
If you eat it, it tastes like lemon.

It isn't luck, it's life
And death.
It tastes bitter.

being normal

Normal works from nine to five
Normal wants to learn to drive
Normal doesn't think aloud
Normal melts into the crowd
Normal laughs at normal jokes
Normal hangs out with the blokes
Normal's reading normal books
Normal sticks to normal looks

Normal isn't weird or strange
Normal sees no need for change
Normal's aspirational
Non-denominational
Norman's normal, that's ok
Ava's average, come what may
But Zeke's a freak and Todd is odd
And Jane's a punishment from God

Normal's limbs all work just fine
Normal sits with neutral spine
Normal's straight, in every sense
Normal's sitting on the fence
Normal's happy with its gender
Normal man is not too tender
Normal woman not too tough
But normal isn't good enough

So normal craves success and fame
Normal isn't quite the same
For women as it is for men
Normal goes to bed at ten
Normal's hers and normal's his
Normal's what it says it is
Normal thinks like normal should
Normal thinks that normal's good

Normal keeps you 'in' and cool
Keeps you safe from ridicule
Cos normal folk are never cruel
To other normals – as a rule
Normal's neither thin nor fat
– Who the feck decided that?
Is this definition formal?
Who determines what is normal?

Normal tricked and normal lied
– I couldn't be normal if I tried

please SHARE

This poor old dear
Lives life in fear
While this snout-in-the-trough MP
Claims a grand a week
It's a bloody cheek
Please SHARE if you agree

Neglected cats
Outrageous facts
Leaders we mistrusted
Shocking quotes
Disgraceful votes
Please SHARE if you're disgusted

Please click and show
That you say No
To pensioner poverty
Bad things are bad!
Sad things are sad!
Please SHARE if you agree

Now tip the wink
And click this link
For more great memes to spread
Join the trends
Impress your friends
Please SHARE to keep ahead

This Muslim bloke
Is snorting coke
And us lot have to pay
Though it's not true
It's a heady brew
So SHARE it anyway

He's not alone!
He has a phone!
He can't be a refugee!
It's cut and cropped
And photoshopped
But SHARE if you agree

This lazy shit's
On benefits
This bloke looks like a perv
This meme is hot
Whether true or not
You'll SHARE if you have the nerve

This beardy slag
Has shamed our flag
And isn't fit to rule
    Come spring my trap
    And SHARE this crap
    Please be my useful tool.

beach body

You all must be Beach Body Ready!
Or you surely must wither in shame!
If your body is flawed or unsteady
Then you just have your own self to blame!

No, the beach has no space for relaxing!
It's a place for perfection parades!
You need slimming! And toning! And waxing!
We have products in buckets – and spades!

You must starve! Don't eat food! Skip those meals!
Don't you even consider a cake!
And no matter how dreadful it feels
Pop a pill or go sip on a shake!

Here's a Beach Body tip that's not shoddy:
Don't you listen to adverts that preach
Because all that you need is a body
Just you take it on down to the beach

Sit on sand with your any shaped booty
Go get tanned with whatever-sized boobs
Know that each one of you is a beauty
Be a man and be proud of your moobs

Take your beer belly, birth marks and stretches
Your prosthetics, your fingerless hand
Disregard nasty comments or letches
We will bury their words in the sand

Yes, right here is a tip that's not shoddy:
Don't you listen to adverts that preach
Because all that you need is a body
Just you bring it on down to the beach.

ranting rhyming revolting

the error of her ways

She chatted online with her ex
    That's where she went wrong
    He showed her the error of her ways
Now she wears a long-sleeved dress

She spilt his drink and made a mess
    That was her big mistake
    She says she bumped into the door
You know how clumsy she gets

She thinks too much and how she talks
    She'd try the patience of a saint
    And he's no saint. She'd better stay
A week or two indoors

She told him that she'd had enough
    That was the final straw
    She won't be walking out that door
Not ever again.

taking refuge

It wasn't like this
When they first shared a kiss
Her heart aches it.
He tells her she's weak
She's a failure, a freak
    And she takes it.

He tells her to say
That all is ok
So she fakes it.
He shouts in her face
So that she knows her place
    And she takes it.

Now somebody's said
There's a bruise on her head
So she shakes it.
But she's made him look bad
Now he's angry and mad
    And she takes it.

She stumbles and slips
And she tumbles and trips
And she breaks it.
The doctor says here's
Something strong for your tears
    And she takes it.

She doesn't know how
She will live through this row
But she makes it.
She walks past a stall
With a card saying call
     And she takes it.

And sleeping inside
Is her strength and her pride
So she wakes it.
She calls and they say
That she won't have to stay
They can offer a way
     And she takes it.

An alternative final stanza if austerity wins:

But the number's been cut
And the refuge is shut
She forsakes it.
She rips up the card
She's battered and scarred
Her life is too hard
     So she takes it.

become not women

*The Philadelphia Ledger opposed the 1848 Convention for Woman's Rights
and urged ladies to stay as 'wives, belles, virgins and mothers'.*

We strongly urge our female readers
In wimples, bonnets, veils and mufflers
You're made as bearers, carers, feeders
Not drivers, tellers, surgeons, discoverers
Girls, stay at home and sew your days
No trade nor college as your brothers
Serve, adorn, keep pure and raise
Wives, belles, virgins and mothers

Philly wants its fillies chained
For breeding mares not running wild
So say 'I will' and entertain
And keep thee chaste then raise the child
Stir the cookpot, wash and pray
That if he dies your living's covered
Turn not into women, stay
Our wives, belles, virgins and mothers

Convert ye not from these to women
With views, demands, loud voices, rights
We fear the cold of homes fires dimming
Sign not this Sentiment to fight
Become not women, darling things
Keep private hells that surge and smother
With bands and rings and apron strings
For wives, belles, virgins and mothers

'Convention' means our fine traditions
Not halls of speeches, fancy schemes
Of harridans who rouse sedition
For 'rights' and other silly dreams
No spinsters', harpies', whores' agenda
A man's firm hand must grip the rudder
Be passive, pretty, untarnished, tender
Be wives, belles, virgins and mothers

thirty five

The life expectancy of a Black trans
woman in the USA is just 35.

Black boys grown women fighting to survive
In freedom's land are some folks not allowed
To live beyond the age of thirty-five?

Dysphoria and prejudice connive
From gender manacles to funeral shroud
Black boys grown women fighting to survive

Must humans hide or lie to stay alive?
Does Pride now mean our sisters must be proud
Of living past the age of thirty-five?

What torment, hatred, bigotry will drive
Her own hand, or her killer's, baying crowd
Black boys grown women fighting to survive

Conformity proves lethal and deprives
Its deviants whose rights are disavowed
Of life beyond the age of thirty-five

So make the change, the equal dream revive
Go tell the world the truth and say it loud
Black boys grown women fighting to survive
To live beyond the age of thirty-five

things I don't have

A crystal ball, a magic wand
Any goldfish in my pond
(That's because I have a cat
And she quite soon made sure of that)
Instinctive urge to deference
Any sort of fashion sense
A strong opinion as to whether
Socks and sandals go together
A way to ward off insect bites
High-heeled shoes or fishnet tights
An LBD or sparkly gown
Much to live for when I'm down
(But countless blessings when I'm up)
A team that's ever won the Cup
A pressure cooker, tumble dryer
Till recently, a deep fat fryer
Place mats, table cloths, net curtains
Floral bed sheets, that's for certain
Enough flat, eight-stud LEGO bricks
The time of day for sexist pricks
A plan, a choice, the time, a clue
Any notion what to do
In awkward social situations
Diplomacy or any patience
A filter on my whirring brain
Mastery of my domain
A patient tongue – well, not for long
A favourite AC/DC song
A skinny waist or narrow hip
A vote for Labour's leadership
A monkey's toss to give on earth
How much your bloody house is worth
A motorcycle any more
A working doorbell on my door

A flawless record, perfect past
Faith in every vote I've cast
An eyebrow-, nose-ring or tattoo
Or much idea what to do
When someone says hello and I
Can not recall their name or why
A house as tidy as I could
A bath as often as I should
A valet, cleaner, butler, chauffeur
Speech-writer, slave or general gopher
Expertise how cakes are made
Investments in the weapons trade
(At least not ones I know about)
A liking for a pint of stout
Telepathy or quite the knack
Eyes located in the back
Of my own head or, being blunt
The proper number in the front
A royal baby souvenir
From this or any other year
Physical co-ordination
Any flamin' inclination
To wait much more for liberation
Freedom and emancipation
The right to get a free prescription
A satellite TV subscription
But I've got warmth and stuff to read
So I've got everything I need

justified

In October 2015, two reports found that the actions of Officer Timothy Loehmann in shooting dead black twelve-year-old Tamir Rice in Cleveland Ohio on 22 November 2014 were 'justified'.

Tamir Rice
Shot down twice
First his life and now his name
Deadly cops and children's game
Loehmann wins
Deadly sins
Bloodlust and pride
'Justified'

The caller said he's just a boy
Told 911 the gun's a toy
Surveillance footage hasn't lied
Restraint discussed? Not even tried
Two seconds after he arrived
He fired his shots and Tamir died
'Justified'

A judge implied
He must be tried
Perhaps not now he's
'Justified'

   His actions were 'reasonable'
   It's barely believable
   The verdict's appealable
   But a twelve-year-old life is not so redeemable
'Justified'

Expert-sanctioned homicide
Sanctimony sanitised
Reports will read like lullabies
While this young life is nullified
'Justified'

Divide and rule and subdivide
Mistrust, disgust is multiplied
'Justified'

Devils blushed and angels cried
'Justified'

Justice brushed aside
'Justified'

officer slager's defence

On 4 April 2015, in the North Charleston, South Carolina, police officer Michael T Slager shot dead fifty-year-old black man Walter L Scott. He is to be charged with murder.

Officer Michael T Slager, how do you plead to the charge of the
    murder of Walter L Scott?

I plead not guilty
On the grounds that it is well established
That it is lawful for a white cop to kill a black person

I plead not guilty
On the grounds of provocation
He was black in a public place
How is a responsible officer supposed to react?

I plead not guilty
On the grounds that he was running away
And therefore obviously guilty
Of having a broken tail-light

I plead not guilty
On the grounds of self-defence
As a white cop, I believed him to be black and threatening
I had to protect myself

I plead not guilty
Under the 'stand your ground' law
I stood my ground
And shot him eight times

I plead not guilty
Not on the grounds of
Temporary insanity
But of permanent inhumanity

ranting rhyming revolting

I plead not guilty
On the grounds that it is well-established
That it is lawful for a white cop to kill a black person
I cite the following case law:

Officer Daniel Pantaleo killed Eric Garner, New York City
    – no charge
Officer Darren Wilson killed Michael Brown, Ferguson
    – no charge
Two officers shot and killed Gabriella Nevaraz, Sacramento
    – no charge
I rest my case

The defendant shall rise
Officer Michael T Slager, your plea is rejected on the grounds
    that
Although it is indeed lawful for a white cop to kill a black
    person
It is a crime to be filmed doing so
Guilty. Of murder. And extreme carelessness.

unpublished author

A traveller to worlds of unvisited places
A winner of numerous unstarted races
A painter of touch-ups that could have been pictures
Designer of unproduced fittings and fixtures
Inventor of gadgets that didn't make patent
Fine skills unfulfilled and fierce passions still latent
A cordon bleu chef feeds her kids what she cooks
An author of several unpublished books

A soul-drenched soprano who sings in the shower
An artist who hires out her craft by the hour
A teller of stories, a co-educator
A thinker, philosopher, poet, creator
Composer of lullabies heard just at home
Her life may stand still but her mind likes to roam
A writer of lines stuffed in crannies and nooks
An author of several unpublished books

A washer of dishes, a wiper of arses
A lister of wishes, a dropout from classes
When muse would have struck, she was clearing up muck
Or earning a buck, or so tired she got stuck
A riser at dawn, she's a clock-in-and-out-er
She's patched up and worn, she's a serial self-doubter
That sleazeball at work says she's losing her looks
An author of several unpublished books

She'd dance in the dusk but her neighbour's abusive
Containerised living is hardly conducive
She'd love to be noticed but breaks are elusive
The one time she tried, the reply was conclusive
A writer of plotlines, deviser of hooks
An author of several unpublished books

A worker of overtime, Christmas is nearing
She's toiling in noise, getting harder of hearing
Watch time grinding onwards, her dreams disappearing
Her subconscious critic is constantly jeering
She's one of those stars whom our world overlooks
An author of several unpublished books

roses and bread

The house is getting dirty, she can't face it
The vacuum cleaner's burnt out, lying dead
She knows she'll have to save up to replace it
She wants a life of roses not just bread
And sucking up the dust from crusty carpets
Is never going to give her quite the pleasure
Of thumbing dusty pages at the markets
To clear the cranial cobwebs seeking treasure
    She finds herself a smart and clean manoeuvre
    The bookshelves are all full now in the backroom
    And stacks of volumes standing in the shed
    'Cos though she knows she really needs a hoover
    Each time she has the money for a vacuum
    She buys herself a book to read instead

superwoman

I couldn't be Leia Organa 'cos
I could not pull off 'Princess'
I could not do the pucker scene
With Luke – that's on-screen incest!
Queen Amidala's not for me
She's hardly proletarian
I couldn't be Katniss Everdeen
'Cos I'm a vegetarian
I couldn't ever kill myself
However high the fees
I'm not Louise or Thelma from
Thelma and Louise
Hermione Grainger? She's too young
And as for Mrs Weasley
No – neither all that mothering
Nor magic would come easily
I could not be Uhuru, it's
Too late – that chance has gone
My buckling is not swash enough
To be Elizabeth Swann
No way could I be Buffy –
My high kicks aren't so high
Not fit enough for Lara Croft
However hard I try
>   I could not be a Superwoman
>   Nor ornamental wife
>   I guess I'll have to stick to playing
>   The lead in my own life

the best-laid plans

Drifts here together with his buddy
they pitch up with prayers and plans
A stake for a patch where they can scratch out
a living with their own hands
The preacher says labour makes you holy
your gold must be earned not panned
But nobody never gets to heaven and nobody gets no land

Boss at the ranch house has his treasures
his lady and livestock grand
Bindlestiffs come to find salvation
to save and to turn their hand
But the stairway gives out before the landing
That's seared with the owner's brand
'Cause nobody never gets to heaven and nobody gets no land

I know that our toil earns just for owners
my fancies have long been canned
Shot with your dog when he got useless
and crushed with your dead right hand
Why don't those dreamers ever wake up?
and why don't they understand
That nobody never gets to heaven and nobody gets no land

heroes and hordes

If Nicholas Winton were saving the children today
His Transport of Kindness would camp out in fear at Calais
Compassion is easier cast back through history's mist
Abhorrence for migrants but Oscars for Schindler's List

No humans may cross here, this tunnel is only for freight
Hurrah for the Blackshirts and see off the swarms at the gate
They've kind words for history, now for the iron-clad fist
Coldness for Calais and Oscars for Schindler's List

The lords of the fortress will draw bloody lines in the sand
Armed guard at the border instead of the helping hand
They'll trample the memory of saviours whose statues they've kissed
With borders of barbed wire and Oscars for Schindler's List

haters gonna hate

Haters gonna hate
Dictators gonna dictate
Tyrants gonna tyrannise
Rebels will rebel and rise
Rival rulers gonna ride
Rebellion's discontented tide

Bombers gonna bomb
Pogromists will pogrom
Fighters gonna fight
Families gonna take flight
Borders gonna rise
Papers gonna scandalise

Blamers gonna blame
Play divide-and-rule-us game
Leaders gonna lead?
No, leaders gonna look away
Leaders gonna see which way
Opinion's wind will blow today

Blockade is gonna block
Shocking photo's gonna shock
Donaters will donate
Activists will activate
Humans gonna humanise
People gonna organise

Arms will hold out hands
Banners held by football fans
Reachers gonna reach
Our hands across the barbed-wire beach
Spinners gonna spin
Solidarity is gonna win.

the crossing

Queue, crawl, window down, good day
Who? How many? Where from? Which way?
How long? What for?
Been here before?

Park, get out. Through those gates
Forms, names, numbers, dates
Terrorist? Spy? Crimes to confess?
(Does anyone ever answer Yes?)

Thumbprints, fingers, photographs
Of us not them. Stamps. And pass.
Official, uniform, coat with arms
Crossing, crosshair, cross my palm

Who? How many? Where to today?
What's a border anyway?
Draw the line, go through the gates
Divided thousand island states

ten haiku

A Japanese form
of seventeen syllables:
five, seven, and five

Dreams
> Live your dreams they said
> Naked on the bus it seems
> Is not what they meant

Eleven plus
> The case once made for
> Grammar schools has been destroyed
> Comprehensively

Word of the Week
> Great word 'tmesis'
> Insertion of a swear word
> Fan-fucking-tastic

Quote as Haiku
> 'Freedom is always
> The freedom of dissenters'
> Rosa Luxemburg

Wolf in Sheep's Clothing
> May look cuddly but
> Harms London says urban fox
> Of Boris Johnson

PM-Kus
I have a question
It's from Janine of Hackney
How low can you sink?

Depression
I worry about
People who are not depressed
They must be insane

Tweeting
Restrictive texting:
Twitter did not invent it
Haiku got there first

Tina
Mantras come and go
There Is No Alternative
Until we make one

Blood
When mopping up blood
We might also ask ourselves
Who is spilling it

She chose a day to cast away
The gag she wore on words she'd say
The date was booked, twice underlined
The day she set to speak her mind

She told the shop she's not impressed
With two-for-ones and more-for-less
And fair but firm, she told them flat
She did not want a drink with that
She told the phone she did mind holding
That she was bored of paper-folding
She told the useless referee
That was a slam-dunk penalty
She called out in her dressing gown
To turn that blasted racket down
She stared ahead and did not blink
The day she'd say just what she'd think

She told the preacher at the station
To quit the hellfire and damnation
She told her landlord: rent's not due
Until he's fixed her leaking loo
She told the rental agent's bloke
Two hundred quid a week's a joke
She told her boss she's off at three
So call it nauseous lethargy
She's sick and tired of work, you see
And she's got somewhere else to be
Her frown relaxed, her toes uncurled
The day she chose to tell the world

ranting rhyming revolting

She told a poll that stopped to ask
She has no favourite facial mask
And yes, she knows which way she's voting
So no, don't put her down as 'floating'
She rang up Boots and Goldman Sachs
And told them they should pay their tax
She shouted at the TV crews
Celebs and royals are not news
She threw some rage at Question Time
That joblessness is not a crime
Her deep resolve had starred that date
No mincing words, she told it straight

It felt so good, it felt the best
To get these burdens off her chest
But soon she felt a tad frustrated
So righteous, nonetheless deflated
The rent's still high, her pay's still low
She's still ripped off, they won't take no
Her voice had flown on fading wing
It didn't seem to change a thing
However loud she'd shout or sing
The bastards were not listening
Next day she made another choice
To speak in sync with others' voice

They gave their boss a stern rebuff
The pay on offer's not enough
They told the man who beats his wife
To get the hell out of her life
They told the council in their town
They must not shut that refuge down
They occupied an empty block
And socialised the housing stock
They pitched their tents and made it clear
They won't allow a runway here
And how her voice was amplified
When she and they spoke side by side

They formed an evening reading club
Talked economics down the pub
And then they told how they could see
Right through the false economy
And now they knew their history
They knew a better world could be
She did not lose her solo speech
But used it to debate and teach
And used her ears and brain as well
Ideas to hear, digest and tell
She stepped beneath a flag unfurled
The day she claimed her spoken world

Just before the sun raises its
    head above the parapet
One side of the sky is light
    the other horizon dark

We stand by a tree whose trunk has a carpet
    of decorous lichen on one side
The other side plain and furrowed
    with bare and turreted bark

The road was deserted for most of the night
    but now that the traffic is starting
The middle of the highway is no longer
    a safe place to stand

So take to the pavement alongside the fence
    which is tall and robust and so narrow
That even the neighbourhood cats cannot sit there
    and must choose a side where they land

There's no amber on pedestrian crossings
    there's only red or green
So you have to cross or not cross
    there's nothing in between

Come to the gate where we
    stand in a line
With armbands and coffee
    and 'official picket' sign

This isn't multi-faceted,
    this is no polygon
This line has only two sides –
    which one are you on?

janine booth   33

the gaoler and the giant

A response to the (Anti) Trade Union Bill, announced in July 2015.

Said the gaoler to the sleeping giant
Your ties aren't tight enough
These bonds are very slightly pliant
You need a tougher cuff

Said the sleeping giant to the gaoler
There really is no need
For years I've lain here getting frailer
I've lost the will to leave

My left side sometimes twitches, granted,
Though not much nor for long
Your tethers are most firmly planted,
Their anchor ropes are strong

Said the gaoler, you may rarely peep
And only yawn or snore
But I live in fear that though you sleep
You may wake up and roar

Of course you have the right to move
For fidgeting or yawning
But just if my new laws approve
And you give two weeks warning

Said the giant's body to its head
It's time that you woke up
The days have passed for playing dead
Come smell this coffee cup

I've been imprisoned far too long
Though I have done no crime
The gaoler's yoked my muscles strong
And worked me overtime

I am your feet that stand in line
Your hands that sow the seed
I am your heart, your guts, your spine –
Your job is just to lead

Said the gaoler to the giant's backside
You see those limbs my way
If I allow my grip to slide
They might disrupt your day

You may be late or miss your flight
Your gaffer might be cross
So damn that hand that wants to fight
Instead of serve the boss

And if you're prone to sympathise
Or give in to the mob
We have supplies of spare behinds
To do your dirty job

Said the giant's body to its brains
Don't be talked to like an ass
Let's flex our muscles, break these chains
And rouse the working class

Said giant to gaoler, you've had your day
No longer shackle me
And tore those paper chains away
And strode out to be free

Said the poet, the moral of my story
Now I've told my tale at length
Heed not an asshole nor a Tory
Rise up and use our strength

janine booth

island dancers

Written in support of the campaign by RMT and others to stop the Scottish government privatising the Caledonian MacBrayne ferry services.

Our Cally Mac's for sale
Public service coffin's nail
We'll nae let fares go skywards
– Pirates!

Piranhas 'neath the waves
Lurk hungry in the caves
We've seen your profit figures
– Gold diggers!

Auctioneers in Holyrood
Have caught a firesale mood
We say nae island dancers
– Chancers!

sonnet to a bricked-up window

*Mourning the closure of
ticket offices on London Underground
and elsewhere.*

Oh ticket office, ticket office, why
Is your fair window really gone for good?
However much I touch or hard I try
The robot can not serve me like you could
If you had closed 'cause I don't have to pay
If transport were a public service, free
I'd no more need to use you anyway
Nor miss your glazed familiarity
    But still the faceless charge a fortune fare
    Top up, touch in, don't clash with that machine
    Oh ticket office, now that you're not there
    The pers'nal touch is lost to some touch screen
    I'm human and I'm needy, I confess
    My journey is now human contactless

health and safety gone mad

Those hard hats and safety equipment
Are for wusses not real working blokes
So go unload that hazardous shipment
If you die we'll explain to your folks

No, we won't spend our cash on protection
Our company has to compete
We don't mind if you catch an infection
As long as you die on your feet

So why do your children look sad today?
Your injury isn't that bad
It's health and safety gone mad, I say
It's health and safety gone mad

Now they won't let our children play conkers!
Or sport without full body armour!
I tell you, the world's going bonkers
A few blows round the head never harm you

I know all these stories are kosher
They're here in the Daily Express
They're even producing a brochure
On a thing that they call 'workplace stress'

It weren't like this when I was a lad, no way
When that scaffold collapsed on my dad
It's health and safety gone mad, I say
It's health and safety gone mad

This happened when red politicians
Gave in to the union mob
Let's return to Victorian conditions
Where death was just part of the job

Let's stop all this safety hysteria
Cut through the red tape and be free!
My motives of course are ulterior
Less cost is more profit for me

These mountains of rules are a fad, I'd say
When they're buried and dead I'll be glad
It's health and safety gone mad, I say
It's health and safety gone mad

you

for John Leach

Ageing punk bands in their prime
Winning goals in extra time
Subtitled Nordic TV crime
And watching it with you

Singing Set the House Ablaze
Dorset cottage holidays
Friday evening takeaways
And eating them with you

Chuckling at our mums and dads
Collecting pens and other fads
Outnumbered four-to-one by lads
Our family made with you

Picket lines and politics
Getting on each others' wicks
Cats and dogs and LEGO bricks
And fishing reels and you

Recommended reading books
Stupid jokes and knowing looks
Eating what our youngest cooks
And drinking tea with you

Your voice on radio interviews
And swearing at the bloody news
Articulating fiery views
And poetry and you

If I don't always fit you in
Between these many life-warm things
Please know that these and everything
Is filled with love and you

ranting rhyming revolting

Every year on holiday he says
He'll write his life, a memoir from the flat
Where once a letter slipped beneath the mat
And sent him off to work not college days
He says he'll put on record anecdotes
Red cash bag in the office flying high
On picket lines and letterheads and tie
Guitars and drum kits, reels and fishing floats
    He'll write of those who fell along the way
    He'll write of those he brought into his world
    He'll write of victories won and lessons learned
    And then he'll take a well-earned holiday
    Another year not written down nor read
    As every year he lives his life instead

manifesto from behind the mask

Make me a mask so that no-one can see
That the face that I'm wearing is not really me
Get me a glaze to go over my eyes
To look like I'm looking while melting inside

Fetch me some specs that can read between lines
Fit me antennae that pick up the signs
Lend me a lens that reads unwritten rules
Bless me with patience to help suffer fools

Find me a babel fish trained to translate
The looks and the hints and the traps and the bait
Arm me with ammo so I'm never caught
In the crossfire of banter without a retort

Fit me a filter to sift out distraction
Teach me a trick to predict a reaction
Create me a coat like the back of a duck
So nothing will stick when they throw enough muck

Install me a switch that will turn off my thinking
Considering, probing, deciphering, linking
At least fit a dimmer or slow-mo or pause
To turn down the volume or close all the doors

Give me that gift that they call 'inhibition'
So I know when to hush and reserve my position
Programme an app that decodes all the crap
Build me a bridge 'cross the processing gap

Alternatively ...

Make me a world where not every place
Is buzzing with noise or invading my space
Set up society so you can converse
And I can obsess and neither is worse

Where statements are clear and where reasoning's sound
Where some holes are square 'cos not all pegs are round
Where life on a spectrum is not to be feared
Diversity's normal and no–one is weird

Ditch the requirement for all to conform
Broaden our meaning of what is the norm
Change the arrangements, compete rather less
Co-operate more, re-imagine 'success'

Where a living's a right not a gift or a perk
Where we're working to live, we're not living to work
Where skills are acknowledged and talents are freed
From each by ability, to each by need

Design a fresh start where there's room to relax
To think, to imagine, to heal up the cracks
Agree some new rules where we all have control
Of our workplaces, life spaces, world as a whole

A future where fear, hate and bullying stop
A system where people not profit come top
Surely this isn't too much that I ask
But until we achieve it – please make me that mask

janine booth

the king is dead

A poem on the occasion of the death of King Abdullah of Saudi Arabia in January 2015.

Royal flag at half-mast flies
Forgotten victim sadly sighs
Only another despot cries
When a bloody tyrant dies

The great and good will eulogise
Sing loud his praise to blood-red skies
Soft-wrap his crimes in sweet disguise
When a bloody tyrant dies

Jail and flogging was the prize
For those whose voice and word defies
So must we now not criticise
When a bloody tyrant dies?

Keep alive financial ties
Watch the price per barrel rise
A show of grief keeps oil supplies
Flowing when the tyrant dies

Beheaded victims can not rise
To say good riddance not goodbyes
Speak truth through cant and fawning lies
So next it's tyranny that dies.

ranting rhyming revolting

carpe diem. don't stuff it up

Tears of joy from years of anguish
Corbyn's won – by a country mile
Let red flags fly and traitors languish
Nothing wipes away this smile
The tide has turned in our direction
Don't let the cynics interrupt
Democratise, end disaffection
So go for it – don't stuff it up

We've had our times of sad betrayals
Suffered decades of defeat
The Blairite train's now off its rails
Our movement's getting to its feet
The Labour right is none too thrilled
Well, they'll just have to suck it up
But smugness only won't rebuild
So organise – don't stuff it up

The S-word's on our lips again
Socialism's in the news
Take time to listen and explain
Come walk in working people's shoes
Time to blow the blues away
Let struggles rise, campaigns erupt
Carpe diem – seize the day
What's Latin for 'don't stuff it up'?

Don't think one man's the one solution
Don't stop as though the job is done
It's only half a revolution
It's not the end, it's just begun
The time ahead will test our mettle
No poisoned chalice – winner's cup
Let's stir the dust, don't let it settle
Go on to win – don't stuff it up

janine booth

fence sitter

In July 2015 the Labour Party 'whipped' its MPs
to abstain on Conservative government proposals
to cap welfare benefit payments.

They're cutting help to those in need –
What case to vote against?
This is a tricky one indeed
I'm staying on the fence

Scrap targets for child poverty?
My mind is wracked with doubt
Perhaps, no – maybe, probably –
I'm sitting this one out

What's wrong with capping benefits?
Could someone please explain?
There's good things, bad things – call it quits
I think I'll just abstain

Yes, voting No to welfare cuts
Would lead to Labour losing!
So we must show no heart or guts –
My, this is so confusing!

It's been explained to me at last
The logic's mighty fine
To be against, we let it pass –
I'm going to toe the line

The fallout for a hungry kid?
Now that just leaves me cold
What impact on my leader's bid?
I'm doing what I'm told

The whip's my master and my guide
We're called the Opposition
But when it's time to take a side
Abstention's our position

Of course I'll still expect my flock
To vote me in again
On polling day I'll be quite shocked
When voters, too, abstain

differences

We put our differences aside
As wise advisers said
We swept them out of open sight
And left them there for dead

And how the atmosphere improved
And how united we
Now sidelined were our differences
And we could all agree

Oh yes, we said, and quite right, mate
Concur with you, I must
And all the time our differences
Just sat there gath'ring dust

And while we smiled and slapped our backs
No cracks or clashes showing
We never paused to notice that
Our differences were growing

As we shook hands and linked our arms
And marched into the light
Our differences were festering
And spoiling for a fight

While we ignored our differences
Left outcast on the side
Our differences grew teeth and claws
And bit and scratched and cried

ranting rhyming revolting

We heard a chilling, screaming noise
Which cleaved the air, and then
Our differences crashed in and tore
Us clean apart again

So if there is a next time then
A bitter truth we'll face
The side where differences are put
Is sure a dangerous place

And thanks but no thanks for the tip
A different road we'll tread
In place of putting them aside
We'll deal with them instead

push the button?

We have a fearless leader we can trust
Who's proved to us already that he would
Destroy communities for their own good
Burn shadows into pavements, flesh to dust
He flaunts the firmest finger, face that fits
A leader who can make that tough decision
Personifies the stone-heart politician
Choose yes or no to blow the world to bits
    When button push one day will come to shove
    Cometh that cold judgement, come the hour
    You may prefer your lamb dressed up as mutton
    A warring ruler's hate or humans love?
    The last one I would want to have that power
    Is one who says that he would press the button.

how low can they bow?

Respect for war dead is not proved
By the depth of bow you're showing
But by the mountains you have moved
To stop their numbers growing.

Rank corpses carpeted Gallipoli
At Russell's Top, Lone Pine and Suvla Bay
By bullet, bayonet or dysentery
Eight months of folly fighting lives away
Young Albert Booth got out of there alive
From hell to hell, from Dardanelles to trench
No others from his landing craft survived
But joined the dead, the ANZACs, Turks and French
 One hundred thousand gone from those sad nations
 And all for what? A great futility
 Did lives not figure in the calculations
 Of Britain's First Lord of the Admiralty?
 Excuse me if I don't take out a sub
 To Winston Churchill's great admirers' club

once upon a tory time

Despite our crusade to screw the low-paid
And the jobless and sick in our midst
They're parading their crimes in our nursery rhymes
And in fairy tales told to our kids

We just can not pander to this vile propaganda
So my job as benefits minister
Is to go through each rhyme, taking one at a time
And eliminate anything sinister

Let's start with Miss Muffet, who sits on that tuffet
Eating her curds and her whey
Get up, you slob! And go find a job!
Or we'll take your dole money away!

And Little Jack Horner – he sits in the corner
Not paying attention in lessons!
If he keeps on like that, he'll be failing his SATs
And we'll see him in magistrates' sessions

Hansel and Gretel   they're testing my mettle
Those names sound quite foreign to me
A pair of young NEETs in a house made of sweets?
Put them in youth custody!

That Jack and that Jill, they went up a hill –
I suppose that they think I am thick
Saying Jack's fallen down and he's broken his crown
And now he's signed off on the sick

That young goody-goody, Miss Red Riding Hoody –
She and her family are canny
A skip through the woods with a basket of goods
To that wolf in sheep's clothing, her granny

ranting rhyming revolting

And those three visually-impaired mice may seem cute and nice
But there's something not right in their nest
We'll surely find out what that's all about
With a work capability test

An old dear said she'd spent all her money on rent
And now claims that she lives in a shoe
But I read in The Sun that though she numbers one
There is room in that footwear for two

That Little Tommy Tucker, he sings for his supper
Now that's what I like to see!
The stuff of my dreams, in my new workfare schemes
He'll be picking up litter for tea

Little Bo Peep has lost her sheep
So she'll get a benefits sanction
But good Old King Cole can stay on the dole
Cos he lives in a fucking great mansion

He's paying his page less than minimum wage
And exploiting his fiddlers three
His morals are lax, he avoids paying tax
And all of that's OK with me

So take a good look before we burn every book
And select a true-blue Tory fable
Play with hard-working dolls or we'll send in the trolls –
Cameron, Osborne – but not Cable!

reflection

I vote Conservative –
That's the last time
I tell you.
The reds would wreck the country.
I don't believe that
Austerity is wrong.
Scroungers and skivers
Are the real
Problem. The Conservatives
Will tackle the economic
Mess Labour left. Taxing the rich
Punishes wealth creators. Stop blaming the
Millionaires, attacking hard-working people.
Sod the
Protesters and complainers –
I'm becoming one of the
Long-suffering workers.

> *They're cutting my tax credits!*
> *Taking a vital lifeline away from ...*

Long-suffering workers.
I'm becoming one of the
Protesters and complainers!
Sod the
Millionaires, attacking hard-working people
Punishes wealth creators. Stop blaming the
Mess Labour left. Taxing the rich
Will tackle the economic
Problem. The Conservatives
Are the real
Scroungers and skivers.
Austerity is wrong.
I don't believe that
The reds would wreck the country.
I tell you
That's the last time
I vote Conservative.

ranting rhyming revolting

this be the controverse

A rewrite of Philip Larkin's 'This Be The Verse'.

They fuck you up, Conservatives
They mean to, and they really do
They take away what progress gives
And add some extra spite for you

But they were fucked up in their turn
By titled, landed, privileged fools
Who bathed in wealth they did not earn
And raised their high-born kids to rule

They hand on misery to man
And woman, piling grief and pain
So get them out soon as you can
And never let them in again

the road to recovery

Recovery lies along a road, it's said –
As do Damascus, serfdom, ruin and hell
For some that road is long and hard
For others short and cushioned well

Navigating the road to recovery
Is not just about finding the highway to take
But about who carries whom

The road to recovery we presently trudge
Sees the bling-dripping, overfed, wide-mouthed super-rich
Carried along on a golden carriage by an army of toilers
Weighed down by the unfaltering opulence of their privileged
      passengers

They need a robust suspension system
On the road to recovery
To avoid (or evade) finding the journey too taxing
They cushion their carriage with the bodies of the bearers
Who will bend our knees, take the blows and
Graze our skin on the gravelly surface

Of the road to recovery
Along which it is an honour for us to carry them
They are creating jobs with their demand to be borne aloft!
And their wealth trickles down!
See! There it goes!
A bit dripped off the end of their silver spoon
Into our upturned faces

Throw some ballast overboard!
Shout the well-laden passengers
Gripping more firmly onto their jewellery, gold bars and share portfolio
You down there! Tighten your belts, cast off your luxuries!
You are weighing us down!
Slowing our progress along the road to recovery

ranting rhyming revolting

Don't you understand that we are all in this together?

The lofty passengers call down: Take your medicine!
It may taste bitter, but it is necessary!
So we take our medicine so they can recover
We must keep fit and lean
Enough to bear the weight of our
Ever hungrier cuckoo's child in the golden nest
Along the road to recovery

Some of the bearers stumble and topple into the roadside ditch
The gold-embossed, diamond-adorned, luxuriant carriage-riders
Lean over, look down and instruct their bearers
Leave them! They are scroungers! Idlers!
Living off the labours of decent, hardworking folk like your good
    selves!
If they try to climb back out of the ditch –
Kick them back in!
And too many bearers say 'Yes, sir!'
Though some say 'No!' and reach out a hand to help

The first step onto the real road to recovery
Is to understand what made us sick
Put down the golden carriage!
Tell them to walk like everyone else
We'll carry each other when we need to be lifted
Not when some demand to rest luxuriantly on the shoulders of the
    lower orders

Because the carriage, while built by us, is owned by them
As the dip in the road was ours, so the recovery is theirs
Just as the gains were kept private
But their losses were shared out amongst us, but not them

Recovery lies along a road, it's said –
As do Damascus, serfdom, ruin and hell
For some that road is long and hard
For others short and cushioned well

janine booth

i.d.s.

If David Says
'I Demand Savings'
I'll Deliver Some!

I'd Delve through Sewage
Intimate Detailed Search
Identifies Deeper Savagery

I Dutifully Serve
Ignorance Division and Spite

Immediately increase investigations into illegitimate immigrants!
Deny disabled dole! dock! delay! denounce!
Short sharp shock! scrap social security!

If I've an inkling of impertinence, I'll insist on impersonal
    inquiries
Demeaning degrading dehumanising, dish out a deterrent, dress
    down these damned delinquents with
Stiff sentences and serious severe sanctions as standard schemes to
    sift out scroungers
Instil Discipline and Strictness!

Interview? Dress Smartly in
Italian Designer Suit!

I intend to imminently install a
Duckhouse decorating my desirable detached
Sizeable sprawling swimming-pooled squat

I Don't Support
Irresponsible Destitute Slouchers

I'm inclined to ignore
Doctors' diagnoses that don't
Suit saving sums
I Defy Science!

Indolent idlers
Don't deserve
State spending

Ill? I
Don't doubt
Someone's skiving
Inadequate Dysfunctional Subhumans with
Imaginary Diseases and Syndromes

I'll Detect Shirkers with my
Icy insincere eyes
Disinterested dispassionate derogatory
Steely sneering stare, my
Insatiable incensed irateness
Detests despises and deplores
Such scavenging scum
Impudent irredeemable
Dole-demanding
Sofa-sitters!

I'm irritated by impertinent
Draft dodgers democratically
Shouting socialist slogans
Impolitely insistently
Demanding decency and
Supportive solutions

Instead I'll inflict
Damage death and demoralisation on
Sorry suffering sick

If you Depend on Support
Imagine Diving Slowly
Into Deep Shit, an
Infinite Downward Spiral
Into Death's Shadow
I'd not Dare Sleep

If you Desire Survival
Insurrection is imperative! inspire! include! intercept!
Demonstrate! defy! disagree! down with his dastardly deeds!
Stop the sadistic savage! strike to salvage sanity!

this i know

Jesus loves me, this I know
For the Bible tells me so
And if it's there in black and white
Then heaven knows it must be right
But if this weren't the only book
That I so literally took
Then dragons fly and this I know
For JK Rowling told me so.

borough till I die

I'm pretty sure it was seventy-four
When I first squeezed through that hallowed door
To watch the Borough boys play
My dad wasn't much of a footy fan
He's more of a rugby or cricket man
But that wouldn't keep me away
The terraces then were a boys-only world
Girls who like football were not really girls
It's a little bit better today
In this century, Posh has a women's team
At last fulfilling my schoolgirl dream
Too late for me, but hey

A goals record saw our League life begun
In style in sixty / sixty-one
The record still stands, so rare
Some decent times then bitter years
When free kicks raised ironic cheers
Some seasons hard to bear
But thrice to soccer's stadium shrine
Three times we went and won each time
Three flags show I was there
If you've never lost at Wemberley
You've never lost at Wemberley
Then clap and punch the air

ranting rhyming revolting

So here's to more years going round
Each small and friendly football ground
Cheering Up The Posh!
Please ensure there are women's loos
Fit for human beings to use
Let alone to wash
And veggie burgers with cheese for sale
In seeded buns that are not too stale
And other tasty nosh
And past the scarves and fast food vans
Please play your hearts out for the fans
And make it worth the dosh

Please don't laugh at our bunny mascot
Cos we're not posh like the toffs at Ascot
The big boys need not fret
We reside with pride in a lower division
But now and then our heads have risen
Above the parapet
We stay in the Championship two years not three
So they can't make us go all-seater, see?
I explained to a guy I met
Who asked: with all these tales of strife
Have you followed the Borough all your life?
And I replied, 'Not yet.'

five final haiku

Storms Ahead
>   Weather fine or foul
>   The economic climate
>   Is not natural

Book Review
>   Essential reading
>   Communist Manifesto
>   A work of great class

Announcement
>   Passenger info:
>   Your trains have been delayed by
>   Privatisation

A Slice of News
>   Best headline ever:
>   Circumcision ambulance
>   Found after tip-off

Life in a Day
>   Today I shall be
>   Mostly working and playing
>   And hating Tories